BAD THINGS CAN'T STOP THE BEST THINGS!

THE STORY OF A HERO

By

Sandra Allen

and Shannon Bond

– Dedication –

To Josey and Candi, who taught us about little girls, big hugs, broken hearts and letting go. We cherish the time we were granted with both of you.

_____

Grateful acknowledgement to Stephanie Hill-Hudson, Teri Davis and Gail Garland--- Warriors, all. It has been an honor for the Hero Team to stand alongside you. Where would we be without each other?

Grateful acknowledgment is given to all of the Hero Volunteers who have given hundreds of hours of their time to share a child's hurts and triumphs.

And to all of the friends and family of Heroes, Great and Small, who have cheered us on when the going got tough and filled in the gaps when we were off "doing" HEROES... we know that we couldn't make any of it work without you.

Copyright © 2010
by Sandra Allen and Shannon Bond. 45465-ALLE

ISBN: Softcover 978-1-4535-0386-7

This book was printed in the United States of America.

To order additional copies of this book, contact:
Xlibris Corporation
1-888-795-4274
www.Xlibris.com
Orders@Xlibris.com

Author's Note

Note from Sandra: Shannon Bond is the co-author, not because she wrote the actual words, but because she birthed this book and its message as much as I did. Actually, when Shannon speaks from her heart, her words are simple, gripping and powerful. When she writes something official, the finished product is much like a stuffy research paper, definitely not anything like Shannon. (It's quite sad.) I (Sandra) give words to things of the heart. Shannon gives energy to the words. Together, we are message-bearers. So, as you read this book and absorb its message, think of it as words spoken from our hearts to yours. As you meet the HEROES Team at the end of the book, know that each one of us is "for" you in your remarkable journey to heal.

My gifted friend, Randy Ball, took the photographs. A remarkable child and family agreed to be the models for the photographs. The freedom, the sweetness, the courage, the innocence of a child and the love within this family came shining through in these whimsical photographs. Randy, these photographs are even better than the ones in my imagination. And to my HERO model, you captured the essence of what it means to be a HERO. The pictures of your impromptu dance on the hilltop make the words dance too. You came to this project as a precious gift. Thank you.

For more info about HEROES, Great and Small, Inc. please visit www.youareahero.org

I knew a child, an ordinary child, who was extraordinarily precious, and oh, so <u>very</u> brave. I knew a child who fought monsters who were real and couldn't win... because some fights a child can't win alone. I knew a child who was held captive by a secret too painful to tell. I knew a child who cried in the night and waited for someone to believe.

I believe.

I believe that you will heal from the things that hurt you.
I believe that you did nothing wrong.
You did so many, many things right.
I believe that nothing can hold you back from fulfilling your dreams.
So... dream **BIG!**

BAD THINGS CAN'T STOP THE BEST THINGS!

I believe that you are a promise of great things to come.
I honor your courage with a word that says it all...

"HERO!"

So, HERO, remember these things...
You are a HERO for surviving such hard things
and doing whatever you had to do to make it through tough times.
You are a HERO for showing great courage in the face of such
great danger.
You are a HERO for facing a person who was bigger, stronger, and
older than you when you were so small and scared.
You are a HERO for facing a person who lied and pretended to be a
safe person when other people were around.

You are a HERO even if you believed the lie that somehow you
wanted the bad things to happen. That was one of the tricks that
the other person used to hurt you and scare you. The person who
hurt you, the Trickster, is full of lies and tricks. Tricksters tell lies
so that you will be too scared to tell anyone what is happening. No
matter what big, fat lies the Trickster has told you... even if you
know now that it was a terrible, horrible trick... or even if the
Trickster made you think that this was a special kind of love and
you believed it for awhile... NOTHING the Trickster has done wrong
is EVER the HERO'S fault! NOTHING. NO WAY. NEVER. Got it?

Hold your head high.
You are not to blame for what Tricksters do!

You are a HERO for finding the words to tell someone the things that have happened to you. You are a HERO even if there are some things that are still too hard to say, so you only told part of your story.

You are a HERO even if it took you a long, long time to tell someone what was happening to you. You are a HERO even if you have **never** told anyone what has happened to you and who hurt you. Some HEROES don't feel safe enough to tell.

Telling is a hard thing.

Somebody in your life will be watching out for you and is sensing that things are not okay in your life. That person, your Rescuer, will be close by. Rescuers know who to tell and how to keep you safe from harm. It will surprise and delight you how many Rescuers come into your life to help you heal.

You are a HERO even if you tried to tell and no one believed you.

Not everyone will be ready to hear what you have to say. That hurts. And not every person will believe you. That hurts too. The person who doesn't believe you can make you feel small and stupid with strong, hurting words. But you will learn healing words from people who know that you told the truth. The power of the hurting words will get smaller and smaller and smaller until you can't hear them anymore. Healing words are LOUDER and STRONGER than hurting words!

You are a HERO even if you can't find the one who is watching over you. It is a big thing to trust anyone with a secret so big. It is a sad thing to feel so alone and scared. You are a HERO even if you are all grown up and no one knows the truth but you. You are safe now. It feels good to be safe.

While you are learning HERO WORDS, your feelings may be topsy-turvy and upside down. Some days you feel like dancing. Some days you feel sad. Some days you wish you could go far, far away. Some days you want to curl up into a snug little HERO ball. Some days you want to kick something... hard! Some days you wish you were invisible. And some days you want to shout from the top of a high mountain, words so loud that they echo around you.

HEROES have all kinds of healing feelings.

So, HERO, these words are for you. Say them aloud when you go through tough times. Shout them from the top of a high mountain so that everyone will hear their echoes calling out the truth, reaching other HEROES who are learning them too. As you keep saying them, they grow **bigger** and **bigger** and multiply over and over until they crowd out **all** of the bad things.

COURAGE   PROMISES   HEALING

STRENGTH   SAFETY

HOPE

BELIEVING   DREAMS

You are everything that is PURE in this world... everything that is NOBLE... everything that is BRAVE... everything that is RIGHT. Without you, this world would have lost someone precious. The Trickster could not rob you of your value. These things... the STRENGTH, the COURAGE, the PURITY, the INNOCENCE... these things shine even brighter now.

You are restored. You are a child rescued.

You are changed.

You can see sadness and fear in other people because you have lived it in yourself. You know when danger is near because you sensed it when nobody else did. You know what the truth is because you have heard someone tell a lie. You know what total, complete happiness feels like because you have felt total, complete despair. You know a place of safety. You know the sweet feeling of peace. You recognize courage in the most unlikely of places.

You know that help always comes.
You know that strength comes when you think there is none left.
You know that hope never dies.

All that is **precious** is still there,
All that is **noble** is still there,
All that is **brave** is still there,
All that is **right** is still there.

Some things can NEVER be taken from you.

Remember this,

Wherever you go,

Whatever you do,

YOU ARE A HERO!!!

BAD THINGS CAN'T STOP THE BEST THINGS!!!

The HEROES Team

The HERO Team is a bunch of creative, upbeat, offbeat, playful, compassionate lovers of children. In 1990, the professional lives of several of us kept intersecting as we each took a different role in helping children and families who had been devastated by sexual abuse. That's when it all began. None of us had any idea that we would be launching a non-profit, HEROES, Great and Small, Inc. Our strength is in our unity. Our message is hope. The HERO Team has had the privilege of coming alongside over 1600 children since we began!

In 1990 in Rome, Georgia, Heroes, Great and Small was born...

Janet Burch Baker, a gracious Southern lady, had the dream that birthed HEROES. Janet is the rare person who is as beautiful on the inside as she is on the outside. She has a love for the littlest HEROES... the rascally, the better. Janet is the heart of HEROES. She prefers to be in the background, but excels when she steps out. Janet is a natural storyteller, finds great value in the people around her, and is the friend that everyone wishes they had. Janet sparked an enthusiasm in this community that goes on and on.

Sandra Allen... I am the free-spirited, children's writer, who finally said, "I'll do it" after hearing Janet's plea on behalf of "her" kids. I am the voice of HEROES. I create healing activities for the kids and write all things HERO. I am great at "spontaneous," but not so much at "organization." Jeanne has gently taught me that people *like* clear directions and cannot read my mind.

What's up with that? Other Life Lessons Learned from the HERO Team: We energize each other. We are better together than separately. And laughter is the best sound in the world.

Jeanne Alshouse, warm and compassionate, is the soul of HEROES. She is a wonderful blend of creativity, professionalism, calmness, laughter and tears. Jeanne is an administrator extraordinaire and a quiet leader, who leads by serving. Jeanne makes things pretty... whether it is choosing fonts and colors for this book, organizing events, or adding the special details that turn average things into spectacular things. Jeanne's experiences and wisdom help us untangle problems and set our course. Jeanne has retired and relocated to Rome, Georgia, to do Heroes.

Tina Bartleson, loyal and courageous, organizes us and keeps us ever-moving forward. She is the anchor of HEROES. Tina is a diplomat by nature, but a force to be reckoned with if a child is threatened. Tina doesn't back down. She is the soft-spoken leader who can take monumental tasks and break them down into manageable "to do" lists. Tina has the ability to spot potential problems without being negative. We count on her to protect us from doing things before we have seen the big picture.

Shannon Bond, our warrior, believes the children and they know it. Her enthusiasm and passion are contagious. Shannon is the protector, the strength of HEROES. She's the queen of drama and the mother of a wonderful puppet named Hermena Belle. Shannon and Hermena Belle have taught safety skills to hundreds of children. Along with bringing puppets to life, Shannon teaches, coaxes, cajoles, motivates and encourages people to believe in themselves and to face danger head-on and with a plan. Shannon has been co-creating activities with Sandra for the last several years. She is a natural advocate, fearless, bold and confident.

Ted Buckenham, the quiet mischief-maker and photographer, is always ready to play and be a goofball for the sake of the children. Ted is the techno whiz. We suspect that he is brilliant, but no one knows for sure. Ted is the message of HEROES. His commitment and dedication kept HEROES afloat through some tough times. We call him "Mr. Hero." Ted is methodical and practical, even when he is having fun. He loves gadgets, toys, stupid jokes and silly songs. He is NOT the token male for HEROES, so if he tells you differently, it is a lie. The kids love partnering with Ted. He speaks their language... and that's all I will say about that.

When the HERO Team embarked on this journey, we never knew that it was our lives that would be forever changed. God bless us one and all.

From left to right: Sandra Allen, Tina Bartleson, Jeanne Alshouse, Janet Baker, Shannon Bond, Ted Buckenham

A portion of the proceeds from sales of this book will go to Heroes, Great and Small, Inc. For more information about HEROES, Great and Small, Inc., please visit www.youareahero.org

Printed in the United States
by Baker & Taylor Publisher Services